LET'S FIND OUT! PRIMARY SOURCES

GUTENBERG'S BIBLE

JASON CARTER

Britannica
Educational Publishing

IN ASSOCIATION WITH

ROSEN
EDUCATIONAL SERVICES

Published in 2017 by Britannica Educational Publishing (a trademark of Encyclopædia Britannica, Inc.) in association with The Rosen Publishing Group, Inc.
29 East 21st Street, New York, NY 10010

Distributed exclusively by Rosen Publishing.
To see additional Britannica Educational Publishing titles, go to rosenpublishing.com.

First Edition

Britannica Educational Publishing
J.E. Luebering: Executive Director, Core Editorial
Mary Rose McCudden: Editor, Britannica Student Encyclopedia

Rosen Publishing
Nicholas Croce and Amelie von Zumbusch: Editors
Nelson Sá: Art Director
Nicole Russo: Designer
Cindy Reiman: Photography Manager
Bruce Donnola: Photo Researcher

Library of Congress Cataloging-in-Publication Data

Names: Carter, Jason (Children's author), author.
Title: Gutenberg's Bible / Jason Carter.
Description: First edition. | New York : Britannica Educational Publishing in
  association with Rosen Educational Services, 2017. | Series: Let's find
  out! Primary sources | Includes bibliographical references and index.
Identifiers: LCCN 2016021837 | ISBN 9781508104032 (library bound)
  | ISBN 9781508104049 (pbk.) | ISBN 9781508103233 (6-pack)
Subjects: LCSH: Gutenberg, Johann, 1397?–1468—Juvenile literature. |
  Printers—Germany—Biography—Juvenile literature. |
  Printing—History—Origin and antecedents—Juvenile literature.
Classification: LCC Z126.Z7 C29 2017 | DDC 686.2092—dc23
LC record available at https://lccn.loc.gov/2016021837

Manufactured in China

Photo credits: Cover, p. 1 Jorg Hackemann/Shutterstock.com; pp. 4, 22 Universal Images Group/Getty Images; p. 5 Jeff Greenberg/ age fotostock/SuperStock; p. 6 Rare Book and Manuscript Library/University of Pennsylvania; p. 7 © Peter Horree/Alamy Stock Photo; p. 8 Hulton Archive/Getty Images; pp. 9, 10, 19, 21 Universal History Archive/Universal Images Group/Getty Images; p. 11 The Art Archive/SuperStock; p. 12 © Georgios Kollidas/Fotolia; p. 13 Encyclopædia Britannica, Inc.; p. 14 PHAS/Universal Images Group/ Getty Images; p. 15 © Lebrecht Music and Arts Photo Library/Alamy Stock Photo; p. 16 Private Collection/Bridgeman Images; pp. 17, 24 Print Collector/Hulton Archive/Getty Images; p. 18 AdstockRF; p. 20 Graphic House/EB Inc.; p. 23 Private Collection/Ken Welsh/ Bridgeman Images; p. 25 Universitatsbibliothek, Gottingen, Germany/Bildarchiv Steffens/Bridgeman Images; p. 26 Chronicle/Alamy Stock Photo; p. 27 Private Collection/© Look and Learn/Bridgeman Images; p. 28 Horacio Villalobos/Corbis News/Getty Images; p. 29 epa european pressphoto agency b.v./Alamy Stock Photo; interior pages background image Tischenko Irina/Shutterstock.com.

CONTENTS

PRIMARY SOURCES

Primary sources are the raw materials of history. They can include books, news articles, photos, official documents, diaries, and recordings. They serve as original sources of information about a topic of study. For example, the U.S. Constitution is a primary source. A book written about the Constitution would be considered a secondary source. Some artifacts can be primary sources as well. Artifacts are objects created by people. Artifacts are important for what they teach about the past.

This book from the fifteenth century is a primary source.

Many books in libraries and bookstores are secondary sources.

The Gutenberg Bible, for example, is one of many copies of the Bible. It is important because it was the first book to be printed in Europe.

Primary sources are important for many reasons. They give us direct information about people, places, and events of the past. They can provide historical knowledge that other sources cannot. They can also allow us to have a more direct experience of history.

COMPARE AND CONTRAST

Can you come up with several examples of primary sources? Can you think of any secondary sources for each example? How are the primary sources different from the secondary sources?

THE GUTENBERG BIBLE

Many religions have books that they hold sacred. The Bible is an important book to both Jews and Christians. The Bible of Judaism is different from the Bible of Christianity, even though they both contain some of the same writings. The Christian Bible is made up of the Old Testament and the New Testament.

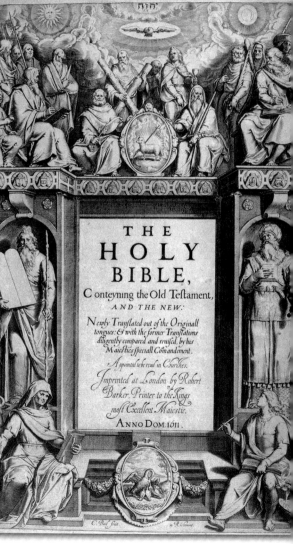

This King James Version, from 1611, is one of many versions of the Bible.

One of the most special copies of the Christian Bible is the Gutenberg Bible. A man named Johannes Gutenberg created it more than 500 years ago. To produce his Bible, he invented a new method of printing. He used **movable type** and a machine called a printing press. The Gutenberg Bible was the first complete book printed using movable type. It marked the beginning of a revolution in communication and the spread of human knowledge. Today, there are forty-eight surviving copies of the Gutenberg Bible. They are among the world's most valuable books.

The Gutenberg Bible is an important book that changed the world.

THE EARLY HISTORY OF BOOKS

Before the printing press was invented, the process of creating books was very slow. A single book could take months or even years to finish. This is because each book was copied by hand, a single page at a time. Most books created during this time were made by monks or professional copyists. They used special pens that needed to be dipped in ink.

Most of the books created before the 1450s were Bibles or other religious works. Along with text, many of these early books

Copying books by hand is a slow process.

THINK ABOUT IT

Monks used to copy entire books by hand. How long do you think it would take you to copy this entire book by hand?

This fifteenth-century illuminated manuscript is called the *Belles Heures* (*Beautiful Hours*).

contained illustrations. Some of these images were very complex. Common illustrations included flowers, vines, and religious scenes. In some early books, illustrations were decorated with actual silver or gold. These colorful books are known as illuminated manuscripts.

How the Printing Press Changed the World

Since they took months to create, hand-printed books were very expensive. Illuminated manuscripts decorated with gold and silver were even more costly. Only the richest people could afford to own books. Because most people could not afford to own books, very few ordinary people learned how to read.

By using movable type and a printing press, Gutenberg could make books much more quickly

Illuminated manuscripts were too expensive for all but the wealthiest people. This one was made for Jean de France, the Duc de Berry.

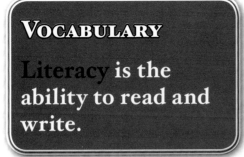

than monks could. A printing press could produce multiple books in a week. This allowed Gutenberg and others to produce many more books at much lower costs. It also allowed ordinary people to buy books. As a result, **literacy** rates began to rise. Higher literacy rates meant that knowledge began to spread rapidly among the masses.

After the invention of the printing press, more people began to buy books.

JOHANNES GUTENBERG'S EARLY LIFE

Johannes Gutenberg was born in Mainz, in what is now Germany, in the late 1300s. His father worked as manager at a mint, where metal coins were made and stamped with special designs. He was very wealthy. Johannes and his family lived in a large and comfortable house. However, little is known about his

An artist's imagining of Johannes Gutenberg. There are no portraits of Gutenberg from his own time.

THINK ABOUT IT

As an adult, Johannes Gutenberg invented movable type made from metal. What were some of his childhood experiences that could have prepared him to make this invention?

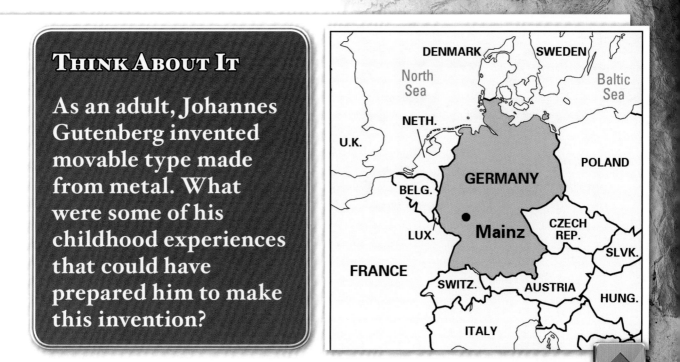

actual childhood. We do know that he learned to work with metal at a young age. It is likely that he learned these skills from visiting the mint.

When Gutenberg was about thirteen, some residents of Mainz began to fight. Many residents were angry at families with more money and power. Gutenberg's family was forced to leave town.

Mainz is in what is now central Germany. In Gutenberg's time, Germany was not yet a country.

Invention of the Printing Press

As a young man, Gutenberg moved from Mainz to Strassburg (now Strasbourg, France). In Strassburg, he began working in secret on his new printing process. Using his metalworking skills, he experimented with creating small letters out of lead. The individual letters could be arranged to form words and sentences. They could be rearranged later to form different words for different printings.

Gutenberg lived in Strassburg for many years. The city later became a part of France.

A worker pulls a long wooden handle on a printing press to press ink on to paper.

Gutenberg was not the first person to use movable type. However, he also invented a machine that pressed paper against the type. This allowed him to print many words on a page very quickly. During Gutenberg's time, machines existed for pressing grapes into wine, for pressing tree pulp into paper, and for **bookbinding**. To create his new printing press, Gutenberg borrowed designs from these existing machines. His printing process is considered one of the world's greatest inventions.

How Gutenberg's Printing Process Worked

Arranging small pieces of metal type was one of the first steps in Gutenberg's printing process. To set type, workers picked out movable type from a case. The case held many copies of every letter in the alphabet. Using these letters, workers spelled out words and sentences. The type was then placed on a flat wooden plate called the lower platen.

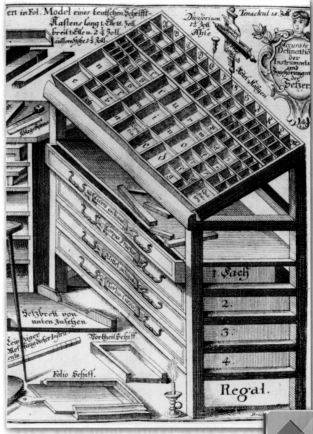

Cases held many pieces of movable type arranged by letter. This engraving of a type case is from the sixteenth century.

In this image workers select, arrange, and print with moveable type (*from left to right*).

After using a roller to spread ink across the type, workers laid a blank sheet of paper on top. An upper platen was then lowered to meet the lower platen. The two plates pushed the paper and inked type together. This action pressed the ink onto the paper. The result was a full page of text. They could print 250 pages per hour this way.

COMPARE AND CONTRAST

Gutenberg's press could print 250 pages per hour. Compare and contrast Gutenberg's press with a modern computer printer. Are electronic printers much faster than Gutenberg's press?

CREATION OF THE GUTENBERG BIBLE

By 1448 Gutenberg had moved back to Mainz. That year his printing press was close to complete. The oldest-known printings credited to Gutenberg are from around this time. They are a German poem and a document known as *Calendar for 1448.* Gutenberg continued to improve his printing technique but needed many expensive tools and materials.

To honor Gutenberg's achievements, the city of Mainz created the Gutenberg Museum.

THINK ABOUT IT

Gutenberg's major goal was to print a Bible. Why do you think he printed a calendar before creating the Gutenberg Bible?

To achieve his goals, Gutenberg went into business with a rich man named Johann Fust around 1450. Fust gave Gutenberg a large amount of money to help improve his press.

The Gutenberg Bible was printed over the years 1453–1455. The new printing press worked so well that the basic method was not improved upon for more than 300 years.

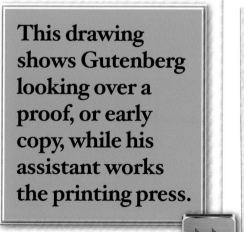

This drawing shows Gutenberg looking over a proof, or early copy, while his assistant works the printing press.

A Simple Layout

The Gutenberg Bible is a very beautiful book. However, it was made using a simple design. There were no title pages or page numbers. Each page was arranged with two columns of text. Gutenberg wanted to save paper, so he put many lines of text in each column. Because each column had exactly forty-two lines of text, it is often called the Forty-two-line Bible. Each Bible was usually bound into two volumes.

Gutenberg's two-column layout let him fit more words on the page. This allowed him to use less paper.

In this image, Johannes Gutenberg (*right*) supervises the printing of his famous Bible.

The paper used to make the Gutenberg Bible was imported from Italy. Most copies have 1,286 pages. The edges of the paper were a golden color. The covers were made from leather.

COMPARE AND CONTRAST

Gutenberg and his workers could print many Bibles in the same time it took monks to copy one Bible by hand. Compare and contrast these two methods. Why do you think Gutenberg's printing process became so popular?

INK

In Gutenberg's time, most ink was made using water. Water-based inks work well when writing with a pen. Monks had written with water-based ink for hundreds of years. On the other hand, water-based ink did not stick well to Gutenberg's new metal type. The ink would just run off the metal plates. To solve this major problem, Gutenberg invented another important product—oil-based ink.

Gutenberg, most likely with some help from painters, developed an ink that stuck to the metal type.

Gutenberg had several great ideas. He even invented a new kind of ink to print his Bibles.

Workers in a printing shop apply oil-based ink to movable type before pressing it on to paper.

Oil made the ink much thicker and less runny. It stuck to metal type much better than water-based ink. Gutenberg also added metals like copper and lead to the ink. This made the surface of the ink glittery. This new ink was a necessary element for the success of Gutenberg's printing press.

THINK ABOUT IT

When water-based ink did not work, Gutenberg created oil-based ink to create his Bible. Why do you think painters might have been a help to Gutenberg in that process?

Decorations and Color

The text in the Gutenberg Bible is black. When he first began printing, Gutenberg wanted the Bible also to have some red text. To have both black and red text, he had to print each book twice. This made the printing process twice as long. After some test runs, he decided to print with black ink only.

Even though Gutenberg printed with only black ink, many copies of the Gutenberg Bible are very colorful. The red ink Gutenberg hoped for was added by hand after printing. This was

The text in some copies of the Gutenberg Bible is red and black.

done by special artists after the Bible was printed by Gutenberg. Along with red ink, the artists added images such as vines, flowers, leaves, and large letters. They used colors such as gold, green, and blue. Most of these images were added around the **headings** of each section of the Bible.

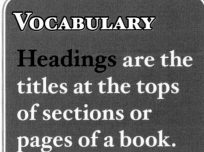

Artists painted colorful decorations on the pages of Gutenberg's Bibles.

A Serious Disagreement

Near the end of the printing of his Bible, Gutenberg and his business partner, Fust, had a serious disagreement. Fust had loaned a large amount of money to Gutenberg to perfect the printing press. Unfortunately, Gutenberg and Fust had different ideas about printing. Fust was a businessman and was interested in making money. He wanted to make Gutenberg produce printed materials much faster. However, Gutenberg was a

The wealthy businessman Johann Fust helped fund Gutenberg's printing operation.

craftsman who wanted his books to be very high quality. He refused to speed up his printing process.

Fust was so angry that he filed a lawsuit against Gutenberg. Fust won the lawsuit. Even though Gutenberg invented the printing press, Fust took over his print shop. Fust and his son-in-law began printing their own books. People once thought the lawsuit ruined Gutenberg's career. It is now believed that he began another successful print shop.

This illustration shows Fust and Gutenberg in a heated argument. The men valued different things.

REMAINING COPIES

Although Gutenberg printed about 180 Bibles, fewer than 50 copies exist today. Some of these copies are incomplete or have been damaged. Several have been taken apart by booksellers. These booksellers sell single pages of the Bible for very high prices. Complete, undamaged copies of the Gutenberg Bible are rare. These complete copies are among the most expensive books in the world. They are worth many millions of dollars.

Most copies of the Gutenberg Bible are now kept in universities, libraries,

This modern craftsman is preparing to print on a reproduction of Gutenberg's press.

This copy of Gutenberg's Bible is at a museum in Berlin, Germany.

or museums. One of the few copies in the United States can be viewed at the New York Public Library, in New York City. This was the first Gutenberg Bible to arrive in the United States. It was shipped by boat in 1847. Another Bible is at the Harry Ransom Center at the **University** of Texas in Austin, Texas. It is exciting to see these historic books in person!

VOCABULARY

A **university** is a school of higher learning and research.

Glossary

calendar A chart showing the days, weeks, and months of a year.

copper A reddish metal.

copyist A person who makes copies, especially handwritten ones.

decorate To make more attractive by adding something that is beautiful.

design A plan or model for building something.

illustrations Drawings or paintings intended to explain or decorate a book.

invention Something made up, especially an original device or process.

lawsuit A case before a court of law.

lead A soft, bluish-white metal that is easily shaped.

manuscript A written or typewritten book or document.

metalworking The act or process of shaping things out of metal.

mint A place where coins, medals, and tokens are made.

monk A member of a religious community made up of men who agree to give up worldly life, remain poor and unmarried, and obey all laws of their community.

print To make a copy by pressing paper against an inked surface.

produce To bring something out by work.

pulp A material prepared chiefly from wood but also from other materials (such as rags) and used in making paper products.

religious Devoted to God or to the powers or forces believed to govern life.

text The main body of printed or written matter on a page.

FOR MORE INFORMATION

Books

Childress, Diana. *Johannes Gutenberg and the Printing Press.* Minneapolis, MN: Twenty-First Century Books, 2008.

Christie, Alix. *Gutenberg's Apprentice: A Novel.* New York, NY: Harper, 2014.

Holland, Rupert. *The Story of Gutenberg and the Printing Press.* Bayside, NY: A.J. Cornell Publications, 2011.

Man, John. *Gutenberg: How One Man Remade the World with Words.* New York, NY: Wiley, 2002.

Websites

Because of the changing nature of internet links, Rosen Publishing has developed an online list of websites related to the subject of this book. This site is updated regularly. Please use this link to access the list:

http://www.rosenlinks.com/LFO/guten

INDEX